The Grace of Distance

BARATARIA POETRY

Ava Leavell Haymon, Series Editor

ALSO BY MATTHEW THORBURN

The Grace
of Distance

poems

MATTHEW THORBURN

Louisiana State University Press

Baton Rouge

Published by Louisiana State University Press
Copyright © 2019 by Matthew Thorburn
All rights reserved
Manufactured in the United States of America
LSU Press Paperback Original

Designer: Michelle A. Neustrom
Typeface: Whitman
Printer and binder: LSI

Library of Congress Cataloging-in-Publication Data
Names: Thorburn, Matthew, author.
Title: The grace of distance : poems / Matthew Thorburn.
Description: Baton Rouge : Louisiana State University Press,
    2020. | Series: Barataria Poetry | "LSU Press Paperback
    Original."
Identifiers: LCCN 2019001726 | ISBN 978-0-8071-7076-2
    (paper : alk. paper) | ISBN 978-0-8071-7185-1 (pdf) | ISBN
    978-0-8071-7186-8 (epub)
Classification: LCC PS3620.H76 A6 2020 | DDC 811/.6—dc23
LC record available at https://lccn.loc.gov/2019001726

for Aunt Patty, Mama Koo, and my godfather Al
up there

for Mom and Dad
down here

CONTENTS

The Grace of Distance

The Call

Once a boy slipped
down a well in far
Anhui. He surfaced deep
in Mongolia, whispering
through his fever
of the vast, star-clotted sky

he swam beneath.
Once I called down
into that dark glitter—
then cursed, then bargained,
then begged—until
someone called back.

"Two Chinese Men Arrested for Stealing a Bridge"

—newspaper headline

You'd like to imagine they did it brick by brick
over days and weeks, bolt by bolt

so no one would notice until it was too late,
the way a lifer might walk the yard
each day, whistling "Relaxin' at Camarillo"

and sprinkling a teaspoon or two of sandy grit
through a hole cut in his pocket, so no one

would discover the tunnel he's digging
beneath his bunk until he'd disappeared forever.
But no. Because this was only a village, once

out of the way but now swept up in the swelling
Shanghai sprawl, and because there's so much

construction already roaring along—
get rid of what's old, tear it down, haul it off
so we can raise another shiny glass tower—

here and all across the city, the sky x'd out
with cranes, who would notice one more

dusty flatbed truck rumbling by, a pair
of migrant workers with bad teeth, no hard hats,
with hammers, bolt cutters, block and tackle?

Who would stop to look back and remember
a narrow, hundred-year-old foot bridge?

There's a concrete overpass right there.
You've heard stories of sheep herders who live
out by the farthest stretches of the Great Wall—

the parts no one visits, that protect nothing
from no one now—carting off loose bricks

to build their own small walls, houses
or outhouses, a brick bed to keep their sons
warm through the dim winter. Wang and Hong

who came east from Anhui, looking first
for steady work, you can imagine,

then any work, then any way to make money,
more money, and now are known only
by last name, only in the newspaper, who

were taken away and may not be seen again—
Wang and Hong broke it apart, loaded up

the sixteen heavy stones and rumbled away,
a Qing Dynasty bridge dwindling to a few inches
of newsprint, an elbow of slow brown river

free now to reflect the stars you can no longer see.

"And There were in the Same Country Shepherds Abiding in the Field"

—LUKE, 2:8

I still worry about the shepherds. Have they
brought along enough food? How tired
their feet must be, if it's true they come from

where they say they do. Two are older,
bearded, in love with the same woman. And one,
still a boy and new to this work, says the stars

would remind him of the holes in his tent
if he had a tent. See how they hang above him?
Some behind a tissue of cloud, some so bright

he thinks just raising his arm
he could touch one and it would go out.

Like Hours of Rain on Piles of Brown Leaves

If this cloud-gray bell's so old
no one's allowed to ring it anymore
is it still a bell? Is the Forbidden City—
open to anyone, all day—really
still forbidden? All mysteries solved,
all bodies identified by the patterns
of metal in their teeth and I'm drowning
in facts and relics, in maps and
audio guides and directions for all the ways
you can get there from here.
Severe clear, pilots call it, days when
you can just see and see and see
but don't get too lofty here.
Only my eye doctor Zak gets to speak
of *vision.* Did you know one pharaoh
had his heart wrapped in cloth
and placed in a little wooden box
when he died? Who wouldn't
sometimes wish to set your heart
aside and close that lid?
Call it the grace of distance,
a starry sky above the pyramids
buried in sand. *Words* plus *temples,*
that's how you get to poetry in Chinese.
And love is *happiness* said twice.
In one day Jay's ginkgo lost all its leaves—
still green, cloven like paper hearts.
Do you believe your heart
sometimes leaves your body
and then comes back?

The swallows must've built their nest
beneath the eaves next door because
under and up, under and up
all afternoon they keep disappearing.

Gray Light on an Unmade Bed

Father Weber with his collar unhooked
steps out back for a smoke
while the small brown dog marks
his territory, sniffs for anything new
worth smelling. He wears the same

name as the old brown dog, who died.
Today's a lucky or unlucky day—
who decides? Could be yellow roses
wrapped in last week's newspaper
or just an old fish. The church
doors closed, that business done

for today. *Thanks, but no thanks,*
Uncle Jerry says, tapping ash
into his ashtray. We watch
the snow fall all afternoon, gray light
on an unmade bed. A blessing,

a few words whispered at dusk
just to us, how little it takes
to make it one thing, not the other.
Once I set a small brass bell
in a hollow place inside a tree
just so someone could find it.

Three Sisters

—for Lillian

Not Chekhov's, but Nauset's
three wooden lighthouses,
moved inland in 1911 and out
of service, so they wouldn't
topple over with the eroding
coastal shelf and wind up
in the water, now are found
here in a field—this pocket
of yellow grass tucked away
in the woods—so we can only
imagine their lights, which
have long since been turned off,
sweeping across the leaves
that wave in the trees to warn
the ships, which are not there,
not to drift in too close
to the rocks, which are not here.

A Speck in the Air

Time for all the words to gather
in my mouth. How strange
they feel, even the oldest
ones, worn smooth by the cold

river, so cool even now
on my tongue. And here's
my only prayer: I send it sailing off
over the trees—a gray bird

cupped, nearly no weight, almost
air, tiny claws prickly against
my palm, quieted under
my jacket. Half hope,

half wish: and soon it's a speck
in the air, then nothing at all.
Is that right? Doubt, if you must,
or believe. Both are habits

strengthened by time. My prayer
goes on and on, to the thin wire
of horizon pulled tight
and further to where it's already

night. A dog barks, waits,
barks again, lost in the woods.
My prayer goes further still
to where the dark turns to

half dark, quarter dark, and now
mostly light. And now it's day again—
dawn picking out the fretwork
of trees, crosshatch of small

branches—the sky lightening
until I can see how that
old brown barn, the one falling in
on itself, once was red.

Your New World

You'll come back as something else,
the monk says, but you won't
know it, and you think, Okay,
what good is *that?* Out the window
you keep seeing birds—well, maybe

it's the same bird over and over
in his gray coat, his little brown cap.
Could be Uncle Jerry. He zips away.
It's spring: the stone Buddha
with bright sun on one shoulder,

snow on the other. People leave
coins by his feet. To a baby, everything
is a new thing, each time a first time—
he's adrift in wonder, the doctor
says—while you stumble along

staring at your phone. Where'd
your new world go? the monk says
or you do. Either way, you feel bad
they had to cut down that old oak tree
but the stump's a good place to sit.

There and Not There

I was trying to get outside my body,
figure out how to leave this
padded bag behind. I don't mean
dying. I guess I was thinking about
the spirit, *my* spirit, wondering if

it was anything like the Holy Spirit,
often figured as a gush of air
rushing through you, a white bird—
you see this all the time in old
paintings—or a tongue of flame

above a saint's head. It's hard to know
how much makes it through translation,
how often what we hold close is
just something someone made up
to express the unexpressed,

but wasn't it always a *tongue* of flame?
It used to be called the Holy *Ghost,*
for that matter, which always felt
closer to the thing, that weird
mysteriousness, there and not there.

A little spooky. Something speaks
through you. Makes you
its mouth. *Speaking in tongues,*
some folks call it. And then I thought
about my five-month-old son

and how late at night, when I hover
over the crib to watch him sleep,
he will suddenly raise his pale
matchstick fingers—his eyes still
closed—and brush my cheek.

Birds before Winter

Dabbing lather across my chin, I picture you: bent low
over the tap, drinking from your cupped hands.

You probably aren't even up yet. Hair a tangle
on the covers, eyelids made pale by the sun.

Sweeping the back step I find a cricket,
wings laced with frost. The leaves keep falling.

I look for you in all the things that are not you.
The plate of milk, left by the cat, sours.

You must be filling the red teapot
with water now, measuring green tea.

The birds wing their way south. They take
the sky with them, each black scrap.

Like a Light Left on for You

Gong Haiyan created the dating website Jiayuan.com
in 2003 following her own unsuccessful attempts to
meet someone. By 2011 the site had 56 million users.

*If anyone ever loved me, I have yet to hear
about it,* says the farm girl turned factory
girl turned online-dating guru. Not that
that stopped her. Her parents wanted
to make matches, not take chances.
But then? Almost twenty-seven! Almost
shengnu—a leftover woman. They were left
to fret and stew: what would she do?
Love, staple us together. Love, gum up

the works. The dowry in Mao's day?
Paid in grain. Then: Happy New Year!
It's 1980 and everyone expects *three rounds
and a sound:* a bicycle and wrist watch,
sewing machine, radio. Or *thirty legs:*
a bed, table, set of chairs. Love
like no money down. Love like the rent
doesn't come due. And you?
I'll make my own luck, she said.
Yours too. Because you want . . . I want?

You want. So the story starts again
the way stories do: a need needed
meeting. She'd help women meet men.
Make wooden matches whoosh
into flame. Because here's fearsome math:
a hundred and eighteen guys fight
over each hundred gals. Women,
you're wanted now: not as daughters

but daughters-in-law. *Honey, is this*
the guy for you? Look at his watch and belt,
his cell phone and shoes. Love like a light
left on for you. *It's not all about money*
but some of it is. Love, unbutton our hearts.
Let the wings of his wallet flap open.
And so busy—here in the city to make
money, more money, how else will fifty-six
million singletons ever meet

except online? *Guys, do you have a sunflower*
seed face? Reliable triangle face? Boxes
checked, fields filled in, the search engine
hums. *Smile, please.* Upload your photo.
Type your likes, dislikes, how kind
a husband you'll be. Two electrons buzz
across the pearly Shanghai sky. How else
can they collide? Or even see each other
whiz by? Like in the movies. Like

wham! Two taxis bash together
on Nanjing Road. Love like hot peppers
sputtering in the wok, like four hands
in sudsy dishwater. May their daughter
someday ask the hotel clerk Gao Zhang
why he married assistant chef Fancy Huang.
Baba? Mama? Love like a table set for two,
for three. He remembers checking
his email at the front desk fifteen times
a day. *Baba married me because*
he's lucky, Fancy will say. *Because I said yes.*

This is What the City Smells Like?

—after the fragrance "Manhattan" by Bond No. 9

No, give me the steam of pork dumplings,
ten thousand made by hand each day on Mott Street,
the cool marble of Grand Central where a quarter-

million people catch a train, shoe polish and subway
ad glue and a pale dusting from the rising sun

of pizza dough spinning overhead. Mix for me
the horsey funk of hansom cabs, yellow mustard
on a hot knish, on-again off-again rain, a dash

of asphalt and taxi exhaust, the sawdust and cement
dust of buildings going up or coming down.

Give me a gust of hot bakery air, the sweet and sour
tang of a rush-hour train—newsprint and armpits,
damp wool, baby powder, a hint of hope

or disappointment, depending on the hour.
For me, it's the dark tickle of luncheonette coffee,

it's briny pickles plucked from a barrel
and the gingery waft of a Midtown sushi den.
Give me 59th Street fountain spray—faint and cool

on the breeze—from that hundred-year-old fountain
homeless men sneeze and dip their toes in

and even a whiff of the glossy black bags

piled high along 35th, trash shining and baking
in the morning sun. But Corsican immortelle?

Gold saffron and sandalwood, notes
of suede? Take a hike up Fifth Avenue and spritz

some other guy with that. Anoint my neck
and cheeks with espresso dust and the grease
of this pig floating past, roasted red and glistening,

shouldered high on a board by two skinny cooks
bickering in Cantonese and pushing through

the crowd on Canal Street. Let us sniff
mozzarepas, disco fries, decades of spilled beer
behind the piano at the Vanguard and the ghost

of cigarette smoke in all the bars you can
no longer smoke in. This city smells like milk

crates full of foxed paperbacks for sale on the sidewalk,
like the fishmonger in her gut-mapped apron,
fish scales glittering on her wrists. It carries the zing

of pickled herring, it smells like glazed donuts
and nail polish, yellow curry, a stack of scratch-off

tickets and a dirty penny, like bodega roses, kimchi
and fried rice and the faraway ocean
you can sometimes smell deep in downtown

if just for a moment you stand perfectly still.

Forgotten Until You Find It

How decadent to pay twenty bucks
and not even take off my coat

and stride past everything else
to look only at her.

But because she was there I was too
for one long moment

at the Frick as my lunch hour ticked away.
Because her eyes, where the dark

paint still looks wet, where still water
gleams in the deep

bottom of a well. Because the deep
shadow her ear disappears in

except for the light
catching on that one bob of jewelry,

because the light catching her
lower lip, her open mouth—she's about

to say or just said
what? Is she hopeful? Wistful?

Reluctant to say which way
her feelings run? Because someone

blew out the candle, someone lit one.
Because she's realizing only now

or for the hundredth time
this day that something won't—

something *can't*—
happen. Because it's all just made up

anyway—"a stock
character in costume"—as staged as

the makeshift turban,
that pale dollop of an earring

(who knows, maybe there wasn't one
more to make a pair

so he had it cheap), so that this feels
like a fable, as if

there's some moral to be found.
How happy I was to stand

halfway back in that circular
dark-paneled room once used for dancing—

as others filtered in, paused, cracked
a quiet joke or snuck a pic,

then drifted out again—and crane over
and around their many heads

to see her face like someone
spotted across a loud, crowded ballroom

and then finally just look
and look

at her looking back:
Girl with a Pearl Earring.

Because it feels as if she *is* looking back.
Because that

reluctance, yes, and because that wist-
fulness. Because Vermeer did

what we all want to do: make time stop
so we can see.

"A rare loan," the wall card said
when finally I inched

forward, while her home in The Hague
was remodeled and redecorated and so because

she otherwise wouldn't leave
the Mauritshuis where she's lived since 1902.

"Dutch *Mona Lisa,*" someone sighed
or at least whispered

and someone else said, "Uh huh, yeah."
The more I looked the less I believed

she was only an array of pigments dabbed
and daubed and touched

with fine brushes
on a smallish sheet of stretched canvas

and not a real woman at all, not someone
turning to look back—

not full of nearly equal measures of hope
and sorrow, bitterness, yearning,

hesitation and wonder and then
whatever happens next,

which of course we'll never know—
yes, turning to look back

as if through a doorway or small window
into this room.

Because she *is* an array of pigments
and not just *an* array but the original array

called *Meisje met de parel* in Dutch
and not a poster stuck to an apartment wall

or a postcard that comes in the mail
and gets tucked inside a book,

forgotten until
you find it and it reminds you

of the woman who jotted a few words
on the back in blue pencil.

Because I thought back
twenty years to a girl in Great Books

I wanted so badly—
clever and willowy, a writer

of course with a wry
smile, who smelled like lemons, liked tea

not coffee and had corkscrew
curls, wide shining eyes, a constellation

of freckles on each cheek and lived
on the second floor of a pale blue house

north of campus I could only imagine
the inside of because

she held back at her door, her hand
I remember never letting go

of the knob,
and said, "I'm sorry, I don't think I can"

because, she also said,
she wanted my friend more and so

I turned away.
Walking the twenty blocks back to work

I thought of a narrow room
small as Vermeer's with tall windows

because one needs
good light, a table and chair because

one needs a place for her
to sit, a place to worry

or wonder and have something to look at
so she can look away—

an open book, a letter unfolded
and refolded and unfolded

again, the news from far away not yet
spoken aloud, a large dark map

hung on the wall and back
in the corner the easel and brushes,

the little cups of paint,
though all these things you must look for

in other paintings
because his focus is so tight here:

her face, her face turned back
to see, her hair

tucked away, just her
shoulder, a bit of sleeve and all else

falls into shadow. Because
the slower time grows

the less you need: a borrowed earring—
"Maybe not pearl, after all, but tin,"

an expert says, missing the point of everything
as only an expert can.

Because light and a pale cloth
to wrap her hair. Because for a year

he thought of her
eyes, that darkness only possible

if first there's light.
Because, finally, just because.

How easy this makes it
sound when clearly for me it would be

impossible. Because
the sun that while I was hoofing it

to the museum was above me
now shone in my face, made me headachy

and I knew I'd be late
getting back, though probably not

missed, and because time
doesn't stop—

twenty years flashing past
like the sleek black cars that sometimes

late at night catch every light
all the way down Fifth

Avenue, their taillights a blur
along the deep dark, the wet-shining street.

Plum Blossoms

"It must have some significance," the translator says of the winter plum, "because everything means something, but although I've studied this poem for years I still can't say what it is."

That winter plum, Wang Wei wrote, *outside her curtained window—
tell me, had it flowered when you left?*

It must have been late January
or February, and he doesn't even say what color
the petals would be. White or rose
or deep red? Cold there, though not
so cold as here. It might mean
he misses her, the way he misses that tree
because he misses her. Sometimes

you can only ask the question beside
the question you want to ask. If the curtains
were parted, you might have seen her arm—
the one that's a shade darker,
even in winter, from sitting in the same chair
in the same spot with the same book
each day beside her window, waiting for

what? It's a small window with faded curtains
set—she often thought—too low, that frames
a branch and sometimes a bird
and lets a yellow square of light land on the table
like a placemat, where her arm rests
as she reads or doesn't read, sips tea

or drifts away and lets her cup grow cold.
He doesn't ask if she has grown old
because they both have. Perhaps white strands
run through her black hair and catch the light
just so. One branch is enough
if it's gnarled and dark, if it elbows out
and hangs low with plum blossoms.

How Every Song Ends

I guess the tune was "Out of Nowhere"
and so it must have been a lark,
a laugh, since the session was already

over, the bass in its case and the piano
lid lowered, everyone headed out
the door for a predawn drink or a bad

girl's arms and don't forget to kill
the lights, but then Joe strums
his guitar, picks out those opening notes

and the trumpets, one older, fainter,
one bright and brusque, step up to tell us
what this song's all about, that time-

less back and forth—what she said
and he said, nudging each other, dis-
agreeing and agreeing about who

was right, who was wrong, who did
or didn't do what, noodling through
all the should-haves and meant-tos

that make up our lives, the laundry list
of missed calls, closed doors, the letter
unsent, that time he didn't look back

but wishes he did, and don't you know
it's late, too late, that's what the trumpets
call out, and yet how happy the end

of this night caught on tape, how lucky
the engineer who flipped the switch,
turned the lights back up so he could see

the trumpets' bells, the guitar's dull glow,
Doc and Bud and Joe—how this whirl
of notes circles the mic—and how

we who weren't even alive for these six
and a half minutes—not long,
long enough, long ago—hold our breath

as here they come now all the way
around to play the chorus once more
and remind us how every song ends

by going back to where it began
until there's only silence and someone
stops the tape, turns out the light.

The Other Side

In the old ink
and brush style of painting
the brush can't leave
the paper until
you're done
so that it's all one long line
that turns and turns and
loops back, taking
its time, and sometimes

standing here outside the door
as snow filters
across the blue-black sky
and I can hear you
on the other side
I can't remember
if I've only just arrived
or it's time for me to go.

Go Together Come Apart

—HENRI MATISSE, *The Swimming Pool*, 1952

Because one day he told Lydia I want
to see divers and because
it was too sunny it was too hot
because it was blazing at

the pool there in Cannes he said

I will make my own

because for a day a few days perhaps a week
it did not matter
if he was old he was ill if he was two
years from death

(you can only count that backwards)

because he wanted to

make color
because this ultramarine

snip out
shapes because with his scissors

pin them to his burlap-covered walls
or tell his assistant exactly
how to because

a collage like a scroll unwinds because

all around four walls
his dining room

and so does not begin

and so does not end the way we must because

swimmers divers swells and bright
splashes

and imagine the thrill because
then irritation
fatigue possibly anger because

an insistent old man

because that comes with being Lydia being
his assistant

all day
pinning and re-pinning and re-pinning

the scissored blue the bright
painted shapes
upon the walls above their heads around

this room

because I do not even know what
is this
supposed to be

because she said because
a wave an arm some sort of fish

a little to the left help me lift it help me
make it the way

it was he said

because water because light.

Before You're Born

—to Preston

To feel you knock
your radishy
fist against the wall
like an irate motel-goer
fed up with his party-girl
neighbors, or to see you
in ultrasound—
      you, half-done
one, curled up
upside down in
your mini hot tub;
the bubble blowing up
in your mother's
belly; her belly like
a water bed and you
making waves—
      makes me think
of pool water; not
diving in, but after
and under, all the sound
turned down and all
that blue light.

A Poem for My Birthday

—after Ch'ang Kuo Fan

Forty-one years have hurried by like commuters
in suits and sneakers, all late for work.
My life, I take it train by train. I keep turning
through turnstiles, zooming
uptown, then down. Whatever happened
to *longing,* you ask, but I long for that

red-barn town where I was born, three states
and fourteen hours away by car.
Now these wiry white hairs, like cracks
working their way across the windshield,
slip into my dark hair. Each day
follows a tunnel to its other end. Each day

a blue memo, something to mail, to shred.
I fly across oceans, eat French food
in France and have twice been promoted
but for what? Wish I'd stayed home
to see my old parents grow older.

The Blue Bowl of Sky over Hangzhou

—in memory of Fong Koo

"Go ahead, *gong gong*," the boy says
once the green light goes on
and the camera's rolling, pulling in
this video I'll watch again later
when I find it online, and his grandfather
says, "An old man feels guilty
that bracken and spring mountain bamboo
are so sweet"—or so the subtitle
will say. His words are Chinese:
they're the words of the Song Dynasty
poet Su Dong'po. West Lake laps
the rocks. I take a bite of *Dong'po ro,*
the stewed pork named for him because
he invented it—the story goes—once
when he was bored, then hungry, then forgot
the bubbling pot when a friend stopped by
to play checkers. And hours and hours
later the smoky aroma, the squares
of pork belly dark and delicate on the tongue,
stripes of skin and meat and yellowy fat.
Not bad. I'm looking for one perfect phrase
to show you this white-haired couple,
this boy's *gong gong* and—
I can't remember how you say *grandmother*
in Chinese—his wife, who stand next to
Su's statue, which stands next to the lake.
He's finished reciting poetry
for now and they look content, they must
be on vacation, I think, though no
smiles, not touching, hands at their sides

for this prim business of photo-taking,
but also a phrase—that's all I'm after
or even just a word, two words—
that catches the quiet hopefulness
of such careful documenting, which says
We were here. This is what life was like once.
Not bad. Now the boy squints
through his camera and takes
a tentative step back, then another, clicks
the shutter once, and once more
to be sure he gets it all in: the liquid-smooth
sweep of rock, darkened on one side
by so many hands, that suggests the poet's
robe, Su's face tipped back to the blue bowl
of sky over Hangzhou—that blue
turning gray, and now turning black—
his long face that looks a little more surprised
each time another camera flashes.

A Huangshan Postcard

The Chinese city of Wuxi ("no tin") was once
called Youxi ("has tin").

That photo of the temple's
cracked fountain—
where were we, again?
And when were we sure
it *was* an earthquake?
Crumbs bounced
in the pie tin.
Glasses rattled—
half-empty, half-
full. A curtain
of cloud hung still, kept
Mount Hua hidden.
Huangshan's more climbable
anyway. A hurt in
your heart got forgotten?
Well, nothing's certain—
except all of it ends. No
painter's tint can catch
that Huangshan mist.
No hiker's tent is meant
to feel like home.
In Wuxi, the story goes,
they dug up the mountain
till there was no more
mountain, no tin.

No More

—in memory of Kathryn Wines

. . . as the blank pages
turn blank again.
—Tom Andrews, "Four Purgatory Poems"

Everything we know will be lost. We know this.

Too soon it will be January, the bird feeder picked clean.
Snow drifting up over the back steps.

As though many little doors, slow to close,
are closing now: how the doctor speaks of her dying.
Stepping over the dark puddle of each period

the reader lets one more sentence slip away.
There is no other way.

The last two deer are so tame—it's all
suburbs now—at night they come up to the window,
bend in the screen with their noses, as if in a dream.

"Kathryn's shutting down," the doctor says. As if
going room to room, turning off all the lights in her body.
"The inevitability and flexibility of a dream,"

Andrews wrote, as if he too had seen those deer.

As if it were he, and not you, who looked into her eyes
that last Tuesday.

Still blue. So little light left.

And I, like an ugly crow scraping away a red berry's
tender center, know just two notes: *As if. As if.*

I lost half an hour Tuesday night to that crow.

I thought: when the berries are gone, the bird is too.
And it was. And Andrews. And Grandma Kate.

The doctor too will one day wander the yard glasses-less,
lost and alone in his bathrobe. He'll need a doctor.

Though I know better, I leave out

stale bread, a pie tin of water, in case those deer return.
Even if it is only dreaming. *Even if*—
a loose scrap of birdsong I'll save for the spring.

At the funeral home, I stand outside the next-door room
and watch a woman sew up her husband's pockets

so he can't take his bad luck with him.

"And So They Are Ever Returning to Us, the Dead"

—W. G. SEBALD

For example, "String Bean Jean" is either a perfect song
or as close as it's safe to get. First the drumsticks'
clack-clack-clack-clack, then that thrumming guitar

whooshes in like a kick to the heart and we're off
with a guy who's got two girlfriends

who've got sleeping bags for beds and favor coed baths
as a cost-saving measure. With me so far?
God, I love that *all night/all right* rhyme, its perfect

obviousness, and that *leccy bill* that's got to get paid.
Dozens of AMs and PMs on the bus, back-

and-forthing to work from anonymous Central Jersey
to downtown NYC, I listened to this half-a-story
of Jo and Phil'—Phyllis? Philomena? I'll always

wonder—and our nameless music student narrator
and how they *get the shopping, have a laugh* and soon

head off to *the cinema*, all in their own language
(they're in Scotland), that common one that divides us
and charms me. Jo worries—and who doesn't?—

if she needs to lose *a bit of weight* and our guy
tells her, *Don't be stupid*—I know, I know,

but wait for this—*'cause you're looking great.* She's his
String Bean Jean, a not-too-happy teen
in her girl's-size jeans. *Seven to eight years old,*

the tag says. *Well, that's pretty small.* But I can't
help wondering what happens next

in that possibly pivotal sixth minute after
the song fades away. What matters most is
what we don't get to hear. This morning

I'm in the dark again. Between blasted scrubland
and gray highway, refineries light up like a fiery city

I couldn't live in. How do these girls grow old?
Cars blur past and I'm half-dreaming of that *house
that's like a caravan,* and of Hilda and her rented-

by-the-room, just-for-foreigners flat in that
row house in Wood Green, the Northern New Jersey

of London, where she got by for a year—
her *foreign venture* when college didn't work out—
rooming with Italian Rosie and Jacq' from Canada.

Christ, this was twenty years ago. With the cheapskate
change box on the hall phone. With wet laundry

strung up in the kitchen and the low bulb I broke
pulling off my T-shirt. With her dreams of seducing
a proper English gent and her job doing something

(I never knew what) on the phone. Her love of *ice lollies*
and the Northern Line, the way she'd say *Ta*

for *Thanks,* her dirty jeans and dirty laugh
and a car crash back home unimaginable up ahead.
For a few lost weeks I wandered around London

with Hilda before coming back to what
I found to do: writing ads, commuting in and out

of New York. Letting years slip by
quick as songs you keep replaying, as if next time
they'll tell you more. Spacey synthesizers hum

and blip and whir and God, I'd give a lot
to be twenty-one again because it'd mean

I had my friend back. *I didn't really mind 'cause
I was fit for once,* he sings. Fit money-wise, he means,
and fit with a girl he loves, I hope, and maybe

even the tight fit of her faded jeans, all that and
anything else you can say before—*seven to eight years*

old, that's pretty small—it fades away. Those days
were quick and fun and then—and then—
and then this strange song is over, all over again.

"Loneliness in Jersey City"

—WALLACE STEVENS

Spite for God, that's what
keeps last year's fruit hanging on
up in the trees, those crimson
berries thick with ice, shriveled
but stubborn. And just what
could have brought you here,
Wallace Stevens? Wet snow
atop trash cans, crusts of blue
shadowed snow and a bird
just the color of the snow drew me
out in my shirtsleeves to survey
this Sunday morning.
You must not mind winter

to say anything is beautiful
if you say it is. To praise slow
slush in the gutter and the half-moon
of ice half-frozen in an overturned
trashcan lid in Jersey City
is a kind of faith. Today
I'm rereading the many translations
of water. First, flurries. Then light
mist, exhausted fog. Rain
in lieu of snow now polka-dotting
the sidewalk, dark gray on gray.
One loses count of the days
tracking too closely the weather.
You too got your shoes wet
on Vroom Street, in the blue shadow
of the armory? Don't mind

this stranger's talk of weather,
this voice in the cold like a hand
that pulls your sleeve. *People*
grow out of the weather. They do,
do they? And after a storm
the telephone lines drape across
the boney arms of the elms.
After this afternoon's storm
I'd give most anything to hear
Lalit Shah's lilting alto, ticking off
on his fingers *coffee, chai, iced tea,*
soda, and also, of course, there is
milk behind the counter of the corner
store he named for his daughter.
You knew it by some earlier name?
Small change. We'll take it. We're
doubters—you'd know us,
alright, Stevens—but we keep going.
After a storm, it helps to hear
a voice in the tired afternoon

even if it's only my own.
Here's a word I say out loud: *Here.*
Here's the dirty glass sky,
sky like a steamed window I rub
with my sleeve. *Come clean,* I say
and it does. Some days the past
is as present as the present.
Two sides to the same pane, that old
out-of-place feeling—looking out
or looking in? Half past five and darkly
falling goes the day and each

of us can only glance back, hazard
a guess just what it is
that's left us. There's so much
I didn't know I didn't know.
And if *loneliness* is only a word?
There are only words.

Driving Out to Innisfree

—in memory of Hilda LaMoreaux

Naturally we zipped right by.
Had to backtrack along that

low wall of mismatched rock.
Drizzly fog. Ben Bulben only in

my imagination. Our rented hatchback
skittery on the one paved lane.

Pretty sure our last turn
was a wrong one but there

it was: a muddy hump in a shallow
lake. Where would he stick

the one-room shack? Keep
the bees? The bean rows would be

short and crooked and then
the words shook free and I saw it

for what it was: a thickety clump
of trees out there. Less place

than idea, a stepping stone from idea
to ideal. That desire to be away

from everything. No sign
even now. God knows, no crowd.

I stood a bit, hood up. Hitched up
my shorts. But who'd go Thoreau

and set up shop there? It still works best
at a distance. Sometimes what we want

is to keep wanting. So—
Shaggy trees? Soggy grass? A dot

of green in sight but out of reach
across brown water puckered

with rain? Check, check, check.
And silvery morning and cricket song

keep you in the clear. Get me back
behind the wheel. Hang out in

the in-between til peace drops into place
like a period at the end of the line.

An Annunciation

Wouldn't it be easier for the old woman
who gets up each day to bake bread
before dawn, who no longer dreams
of anything, and the traveling salesman lost

in thought, perched like a sparrow
on the motel bed, if an angel came down
and said, This is your life now?
Here is what you must do? The snow

like a heavy curtain falls on our first acts.
Upstairs, a teenager sings to herself
by the frost-starred window. Hear her
walking back and forth, bed to dresser,

dresser to bed? Would it be wrong
to imagine these words are her song?
You might suppose she's packing
for a journey, but she left long ago.

Relic

Strange magic, it seems now, a spell to believe
in the candles crossed like swords
across my neck for the Feast of St. Blaise—

God preserve you, Father Weber intoned again
and again. We stood in line,
the whole school, as the white tapers

were pressed against each neck to ward off
sore throats, a lost voice, something
worse. Now, that life's like an old black coat

I've unbuttoned and hung in the closet
and won't wear again, though
I can't quite give it away. I can still feel

my way back to the guilty thrill as I fingered
the crucifix on that worn rosary,
the thick cross with a little door on the back

closed tight with an even littler screw.
It held a relic, someone said—I remember
that hushed voice—a few specks of bone

from a young saint's shoulder,
something I had to see, the pale flecks
smaller than rice grains I stared at

in queasy wonder, tilting the cross
so they'd catch the light—a little, a little
more—til they slipped out and blew away.

Probably

—CARDINAL JOHN HENRY NEWMAN (1801–1890),
undated black-and-white photograph

The cardinal turns. Someone speaks outside the frame. He cups
his left hand—or not the hand, but a finger, two fingers—behind
his ear as if to hear better, or to show that no, he cannot hear.
Is it Ambrose, the younger priest whose grave he'll ask to share
when that time comes? (Was this a common practice then?) The
crisp sharp light, the tight crop, makes him seem contemporary.
But no, this is Victorian England: these soft shades, the velvety
black we peer back into. Meaning this casualness, those fingers,
that shag of hair bright white beneath his skullcap, must have been
carefully composed, a pose held for some time. *Victorian*. Which is
to say their intimacy was maybe not uncommon, these priests, not
necessarily frowned upon—I *read* this; I wondered to be reading
this in the newspaper—but the relationship was "probably chaste."
I want to say this delicately, but *say it*, because I'm not a Victorian,
because I like a love story: a world opens up beyond that *probably*.
It might be the sexton, waiting for the bulky box camera to be
carried away so he can answer. Hands rough from the shovel, he's
embarrassed by his dirty overalls in front of this cardinal who has
asked ("We are men who can be discreet?") for plain pine, fresh
mulch to fill the grave and speed him on: the Lickey hills, that
watery, hungry clay, will do the rest. "Clarence," he whispered,
"I've no wish to be made a saint." Dust let go, dust come home
to dust. Which is why, fast-forwarding a hundred years, the paper
says the Vatican's men, digging in the shady cemetery, have found
nothing. No trace of that sturdy brow. Just a bit of brass, a few loose
rosary beads. And then the mud-colored tassel from his—well,
what do they call that?—his fancy hat. They had to—I read this;
I *liked* reading this—they had to "content themselves" with that.

At Chuang Yen Monastery

Not the moonlit gravel path
but the cool air caught
inside a stone for a thousand years.

The Angel and the Lady

If anyone let you pick him up
he would shock you
with his density, his heft, how

in any weather he holds the cold
deep inside, this water buffalo
carved from a chunk

of spinach-green jade. He stretches
eight inches, neck to rump.
He has turned his head forever

to look back over his shoulder:
a gift from a Chinese duke meaning
spring, that green, a new

year, another chance. Odd charm
looked at or not, touched or
turned to the wall. He gave it to someone

else's wife. Decades, then centuries
ticked by. Until it disappeared
from the record. Until a Londoner

called Sparks let it go for
two hundred and fifty-three pounds
to an earl-turned-colonel shipping out

toward the war. This was 1939.
Wrapped in that week's newspapers
like a poor pharaoh, stuffed

in a crate mis-stamped PORCELAIN,
forgotten when the earl survived
a torpedo but then died anyway

back on land. Decades more before
someone found the box, broke it
open, and wouldn't you love to run

your fingers down his dark flank?
Look him over for scratches
or a patch worn shiny by her thumb—

any sign of that woman who once
held him? How many nights
did she stare at him, Lady Hui,

slip away, slip back, until that night
she couldn't? Whose name did she hide
in his leaf-shaped ear? The way

he looks back, his eyes reflecting,
as you hunch closer now, *you*—
you'd love to slip him into

your sack, sneak away out the back,
but this man would
never let you. "Anyhow it is sold,

practically gone already, back to China,"
the auctioneer says. "But good
story, yes?" He's curly haired,

bespectacled, possibly Hungarian.
He struggles to keep his excitement
in English. "So Chinese people

get rich and they buy back
their art. So that is the story for today."
So—no more mystery,

no more getting lost. Is that why
he's turned now to look
at an Annunciation? He wants you

to notice how this one in a plain
wooden frame, only the size
of an old *Life* magazine, is different:

"Do you see what you are not seeing?"
He's smiling, hands in
pockets, elbows out, waiting for you.

It's a dance you don't mind
slipping into. "Most times it's a tale
we know, the angel and the lady

caught between words—if an angel
explains things with words."
He laughs a little *ha-ha* laugh.

"Imagine today telling a virgin
about her *miraculous* change.
Would she possibly believe?"

You look back at the painting,
gaze at this woman just old enough
to be a woman—a touch out of focus

beneath the haze of a century's
smoke and grime, spider-webbed
with cracks—the delicate blue

folds of her robe, the bright flame
in each eye, her hand closed
so tightly over her heart you wonder

did she even believe it then?
"But what is missing? You see?
She is alone," he says, rocking

on his heels, pointing at the painting.
"The Virgin looks outside
the frame. She *inquires.*

How she questions with her eyes!
She stares back at you. Yes—*you.*
And now you are the angel."

Watch Over Us

—to Keith Taylor

Keith, it seemed only right
reading your *Marginalia*
for a Natural History
on the hot subway home
from work to turn the page—
the pages are loose, the book
well-thumbed—and find
a mosquito poised at the top
of the next one: delicate
as a watch spring, its body
a tiny, shiny transistor,
I thought I'd smush it
with my thumb, but then
how did it get there?
Where could it be headed,
traveling uptown like me?
Lord, watch over us all tonight
on these journeys we may
not even know we're taking.

ACKNOWLEDGMENTS

Thank you to the editors and readers of the following publications where these poems first appeared over the years, often in earlier versions: *5AM, The American Poetry Review, Barn Owl Review, Cherry Tree, Clockhouse Review, Coal Hill Review, Connotation Press, Court Green, HeartWood Literary Magazine, Image, Lilies & Cannonballs Review, The MacGuffin, Machine Dreams, Miramar, Naugatuck River Review, New England Review, The Paris Review, Poet Lore, Pool, The Southern Review, Tiferet, Waccamaw,* and *The Warwick Review.*

Several of these poems were previously published in the chapbook *A Green River in Spring* (Autumn House Press, 2015).

"And There were in the Same Country Shepherds Abiding in the Field" was first published (as "The Road to Bethlehem") in the Christmas Eve bulletin at St. Giles Episcopal Church in Jefferson, Maine. "Your New World" also appeared on *Poetry Daily.* "Driving Out to Innisfree" also appeared on *Verse Daily.* "This is What the City Smells Like?" first appeared, under a slightly different title, in the anthology *The Book of Scented Things* (Literary House Press, 2014). "The Other Side" was produced as a broadside, with art by Kate Baird, by Broadsided Press.

I drafted several of these poems while participating in the 30/30 Project, during which I wrote a poem a day for a month. Thank you to my friend Ava Hu and to everyone at Tupelo Press for this unique opportunity.

Once again, I'm deeply grateful to my series editor, Ava Leavell Haymon, for her generosity, keen insights, and unflagging support of my work. I also wish to thank my editor, Neal Novak, for the dedication and care with which he shepherded these poems from manuscript to published book. Thank you to my friends Stuart Greenhouse and Jay Leeming, who read many of these poems in early drafts and helped make them better. Thank you to the Bronx Council on the Arts for support and encouragement over the more than a decade I lived there. And last but first, my love and gratitude to Lillian and Preston: for everything.

"Like a Light Left on for You" draws its inspiration and a number of details from Evan Osnos's article, "The Love Business" (*The New Yorker*, May 14, 2012).

"Plum Blossoms" begins with an adaptation of G. W. Robinson's note on his translation of an untitled poem by Wang Wei, published in *Wang Wei: Poems* (Penguin Classics, 1973). It also includes my paraphrasing of the second half of that translation.

"A Poem for My Birthday" is loosely based on a poem by Ch'ang Kuo Fan, translated by Kenneth Rexroth as "On His Thirty-third Birthday" in *One Hundred More Poems from the Chinese* (New Directions, 1970).

"'And So They Are Ever Returning to Us, the Dead'" borrows its title from a sentence in W. G. Sebald's *The Emigrants,* as translated by Michael Hulse (New Directions, 1996), and quotes several phrases from Belle and Sebastian's song "String Bean Jean."

"Loneliness in Jersey City" borrows its title and plays variations on titles and lines from poems by Wallace Stevens.

CPSIA information can be obtained
at www.ICGtesting.com
Printed in the USA
LVHW031739310719
626025LV00003B/313